GW00702124

Teach Yourself
SWIMMING

Dr. A.K. Srivastava

M.P.Ed., N.I.S. (Athletics), D.Y. Ed., Ph.D. (Phy. Edu.)
Director, Physical Education
Delhi Engineering College, Bawana Road, Delhi-110042

SPORTS PUBLICATION

G-6, 23/23-B, EMCA House, Ansari Road,
Darya Ganj, New Delhi-110002
Ph.: (O) 65749511 (M) 9868028838
(R) 27562163   Telefax: 011-23240261
E-mail: lakshaythani@hotmail.com

Published by:

SPORTS PUBLICATION
G-6, 23/23-B, EMCA House, Ansari Road, Darya Ganj, New Delhi-2
Ph. : (O) 65749511 (R) 27562163, (Telefax) 23240261 (M) 9868028838
E-mail: *lakshaythani@hotmail.com*

© 2007 Publishers

I.S.B.N. – 978-81-7879-424-2

PRINTED IN INDIA 2007

Laser Typeset by:
JAIN MEDIA GRAPHICS,
C-4/95-A, Keshav Puram, (Near Subhash Place), Delhi-110035
Phones: 011-20296366, 9911151534, 9350556511

Printed by:
CHAWLA OFFSET PRINTERS
Delhi-110052

Price: Rs. 95/-

CONTENTS

PREFACE

Swimming is a well-known sports all over the world. It is commonly known among masses in our country especially during the summer months. Swimming itself is full of fitness exercises and all body plan cover in it.

Teach Yourself Swimming is an outstanding effort by the author in the field of sports and physical education. The art, skills, tactics and techniques of Swimming is briefly explained in such a manner that a learner should learn its all skills and techniques with a little difficulty.

It will prove very useful to the players, coaches, sportspersons, athletes, teachers of physical education, instructors, coaches and the general readers.

The whole book is classified into Three chapters:

The First chapter deals with Introduction of Swimming.

The Second Chapter explains various skills and techniques of Swimming with illustrations for better understand.

The concluding chapter is consisted of all the latest rules and measurements of Swimming.

Hopefully, this book will prove very useful for the sportsperson, teachers, students of physical education as well as for the general readers.

All the comments from readers on omissions or shortcomings would be most welcome.

—Publisher

1

INTRODUCTION

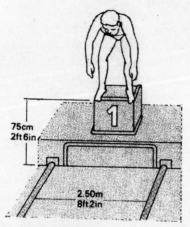

Approximately two-thirds of the earth's surface is covered with water. Of that volume of water well over 90 per cent is salty, which leaves a remainder of a few per cent of fresh water. Much of the fresh water is locked in the ice caps, which means remarkably little fresh water of the appropriate temperature is available for swimming. Swimming itself has widely differing meanings.

At the end of the scale is the person who goes daily into the sea during an annual holiday and, at the other, the supreme athletes who train for up to twenty-five year round. Sadly, in Britain there are areas where swimming is not possible due to lack of safe facilities and, sadder still, are the older members of our population who never had opportunity to learn when young, leaving much work to be done with adult beginners. Saddest of all in one way are the handicapped people, although a national upsurge of provision for the less fortunate is more than evident and some local authorities must be applauded for their efforts. Whether you swim in salt or fresh water, certain principles remain the same.

Body Composition

The human body is composed of many kinds of tissue, but the most important form the point of view of flotation are the quantities of bone, muscle and fat. In a stew the bone and the meat, which is the muscle of the animal being cooked, sink to the bottom of the pot, while the fat accumulates on thee surface. Similarly, when a person gets into the swimming pool, the bone and muscles will tend to sink, while the fat will float. The combination of the proportions of these three tissues will decide whether or not an individual will float high or low in the water, and whether the person will be one of the unlucky few who are classified as 'sinkers', who have no part of their body above the water at all.

Flexion and Extension

Similar actions can be seen in climbing a rope, where first one arm is straight and the other bent, and the climber moves up the rope by alternately bending and straightening the arms. A more formal term is flexion and extension. The largest joint in the human body is the hip, which is powerfully used in weightlifting, and in swimming it is powerfully used in butterfly and also in starts and turns. Less obviously, the hip is used when walking, running and also in swimming all strokes, when the large muscles operating around the massive hip joint can be used to great advantage.

A swimmer who does not learn this, or is not taught it, is at a disadvantage in trying to get propulsion from the weaker muscles which function at the knee. A person who is unfortunate enough to have a fractured limb in plaster, finds it impossible to flex and to extend the joints involved. Movement becomes slow and difficult, with inflexible levers. Slow movement is often used by completely flexible people when they are merely sauntering along. No speed is needed, so there is little need for large flexion at the knee. In the water an exact parallel happens when those swimmers who have no interest in speed, but only in a little gentle exercise and enjoyment, are to seen swimming with long arms and legs, or 'long levers'. There is no need for a lot of bending and straightening, and it should be recalled that it is not necessary because the slow swim they use does not call for a lot of exertion to overcome resistance. However, should the slow walker have to run to catch a bus, he will immediately flex the knees more in order to be able to extend them strongly to grain speed.

In swimming, slow pace often derives from little flexion of the elbow, but those who swim fast bend their arms up to 90 degrees in order to derive maximum propulsion. It is an amusing exercise for la teacher to set a class of children, or for an individual to attempt, to try swimming with perfectly straight arms and legs. It is not possible, but some excited children will claim success although observation will show that there is flexion and extension, however slight, at the elbow, knee, wrist or ankle. This flexion allows subsequent extension which results in propulsion.

Flotation

An important consideration in a person's flotation is the capacity of the lungs, and whether they are filled or not. For the individual who is heavily muscled and who had heavy bones, but who has little fat, the flotation given by air in the lungs is critical, and the swimming styles adopted will be modified to meet this.

For those born with good flotation, the problems are much decreased. The centre of buoyancy, or centre of flotation is that point where all the forces involved in flotation appear to act.

An object falls over when its centre of gravity falls outside its body, a concept important in diving. In the human body, the centre of gravity is usually close to the navel, and is closer to the front of the body than the back. The position of the centre of buoyancy relative to the centre of gravity will decide the natural floating position of the individual concerned.

Weight and Mass

Earlier, it was said that the human body is virtually weightless in water, and in view of the explanations above concerning individual floating positions, some short statement of the difference between weight and mass must be made. A person's weight is a variable, depending on where he or she happens to be. An astronaut is weightless, in the sense that a swimmer is weightless.

Flexibility

Flexible ankles and feet are valuable assets in swimming all strokes. When a person sits on the floor with the legs extended side by side, knees braced straight, it is possible to drop the feet until they are in the line with legs. If the legs are moved apart and then rotated inwards, the feet will drop, until the toes touch the floor. This rotation of the legs is a counterpart of the arm rotation is sculling with the hands, to have the thumb up for the inward press and the little finger up for the outward press. It is to be seen in all strokes, including the breaststroke, where the very best swimmers end their leg kick with a foot swirl which brings the big toes together just as the thumbs are on top as the hands move in which sculling.

Resistance

A skilled swimmer had his body flat, when viewed from the side, as this reduces resistance. To experience just how powerful the resistance of water can be, it is only necessary to be in water of chest depth and to try to walk quickly or to run. Learners, anxious perhaps to keep one or both feet near the floor of the pool, attempt to swim in angled positions. Some elderly people, due either to their personal floating position, or because they lack strength, also swim in an angled position, which creates resistance. However, there is the fact that resistance is largely a problem deriving from speed. The faster an object moves through a fluid, the greater the resistance. Learners and recreational swimmers are not interested in speed and so can swim in a position which would be unacceptable for an expert swimmers, who is seeking maximum speed and minimum resistance.

Swimwear

On the subject of swimwear, there are some important factors for swimmers who race and who have to train for long hours. The suit should be close fitting, to avoid trapping air bubbles which influence the floating position and its streamlining. For girls there is need for a high necked suit to ensure that there is no drogue effect.

Teaching Sequences

The description of the four recognised strokes will follow the sequences used in teaching them. At one time breaststroke was always taught first, but today freestyle, or frontcrawl, is usually tackled first and as soon as the learner is moving, backcrawl is started. Full use is made of dog-paddle, sometimes called front paddle and of back-paddle, or back sculling. At this point usually breastsroke is introduced, swum on the front or the back, and the swimmer then develops rapidly on the stroke favoured most, but continues to develop the others. The method is well known an aptly named 'multi-stroke' and is far better than the rigid teaching of one stroke only.

Eventually butterfly is taught, and for many years experienced teachers have waited until the frontcrawl is well mastered before introducing butterfly. A new younger generation of teachers has arrived which questions the established beliefs and who are introducing butterfly quite successfully after the initial frontcrawl-backcrawl sequence.

2

SKILLS AND TECHNIQUES OF SWIMMING

Everyone should benefit from and enjoy a well-planned swimming pool programme. In order to achieve this goal, the teacher must first consider the individual needs of each pupil. Preparation should also involve a consideration of many other factors, including facilities, equipment, the length of the lession, the frequency of visits to the pool, the physical, mental and social needs of the pupils and the influence of events which may have affected a person, either emotionally or physically. The important factor is that the teacher should be flexible in the design of each programme.

A teacher should endeavour to achieve certain objectives through the programme:

1. The development of body awareness, co-ordination and movement skills in water.

2. The development of safety techniques in water.

3. The opportunity for each individual to derive from swimming personal satisfaction, enjoyment and fun.

4. Interaction with others through cooperative and competitive activities.

5. The promotion of fitness, suppleness, strength and stamina.

The range of activities can vary from an individual simply enjoying the sensation of moving in water, learning basic strokes and acquiring survival skills, to synchronised swimming or competitive swimming skills. The initial introduction to water activities, at whatever age, is of vital importance, but when teaching adults or pupils with impairments the teacher must also carefully and continuously assess the ability of all individuals and their reaction to the swimming programme. The initial goal is for everybody to swim independently using the main stroke techniques, but for many this will be able to establish what selection of activities and teaching methods should be used.

Body Position and Balance

Whilst a person's natural build obviously plays a crucial role in achieving a comfortable floating position, floating is a skill which needs to be taught and adapted to the individual. A balanced float has been achieved when the body is no longer rotating in any direction and has come to rest supported by the water. Frequently swimmers will not allow the body to continue rotating until it has reached this state of equilibrium. A desirable floating position need not be horizontal, although a clear breathing position is essential. In fact, the face may be the only part of the body which remains clear of the water.

An obese swimmer will float very high in the water but may find it difficult to regain a standing position. For some people with heavy muscular legs, this means a vertical floating position, and for a person with more fat around the hips, a horizontal floating position. Altering the body shape in the water can influence the position of these two centres of forces. Lifting the arms above the head moves the centre of gravity to the nearer to the centre of buoyancy, while curling the legs under the body moves the centre of gravity to directly under the centre of buoyancy, giving a very stable 'jelly fish' float position. Archimedes principle states that the more water a body displaces the more upthrust is transferred to that floating body.

Therefore it is important to displace the maximum volume of water for maximum buoyancy. The head in particular needs to be submerged as much as possible whilst leaving a clear airway. With the head will back and with both arms and legs in the water the body is better supported. Spasticity in one or more limbs which might cause an arm, for example, to be raised above the water, results in difficulties in floating, as that arm is not supported in the water and will increase the weight out of the water so disturbing body balance and buoyancy.

The head is often vital in instigating a change in body position, and it initiates rotation around the body's horizontal and vertical axes. If it sinks into the water it may cause a feeling of loss of control and may result in panic. Learning to rotate or balance is an important part of learning to float for those people whose body is more asymmetrical or one-sided.

Even when action is severely restricted, a pupil may learn to counteract rotation by turning the head in the opposite direction. Arm and leg movements can also be used to aid balance. People who suffer from the effects of poor muscle control and uncontrolled, unpredictable limb movements may also experience great difficulties when learning to float. A head support may be needed to prevent the head extending suddenly backwards and underwater.

Some people may find it acceptable to rely on buoyancy aids can create a stabilising effect, and may eliminate balance problems, but they should be used only as a stage towards learning unaided floatation and balance. Having assessed the swimmer's ability to float it is necessary to assess the limb movement. In swimming, propulsion is gained from the arms and legs acting as levers, and from the hands and feet acting as paddles. For swimmers with limited mobility in the shoulders and hips, movement through the water is still possible if good sculling actions are taught, maximising the available movement to give a propeller-type action and using and flexibility of the hands and feet. The co-ordinating of movements is also important for, though isolated limb movements may be performed satisfactorily , the skill may break down when combined with movements of the other limbs. The teacher can test the range of movement by asking the swimmer to move each limb joint by joint. If it is feasible, observe these movements when the swimmer is in the water and as relaxed as possible, perhaps using artificial aids or a partner to help balance.

However, the aids must not inhibit the range of movement. As the arms the greatest propulsion in most strokes, begin by assessing the movement potential in the upper limb girdle. To assess the shoulder joint, the pupil must be asked whether the arm can be stretched above the head. The teacher should note how close the upper arm is to the ear, as this will indicate the suitable entry point for an arm stroke. It should then be assessed how far behind and in front of the body the arm can be taken, as this will indicate whether out of water arm recoveries require adaptation. The pupil should be asked to take the arm out to the side and across the body. Are these shoulder joint movements performed easily and with relaxation or are they forced and involving associated movements of the trunk? In assessing the elbow joint the teacher should establish whether there is a full range of flexion and extension. This should be tested out of the water and then under the water to assess if the movement is possible against water resistance. Maximum propulsion is achieved from a bent elbow action, but a slower yet satisfactory swimming stroke may use little flexion in the elbow.

The teacher must also establish how much flexion and extension there is in the wrist joint, how much sideways flexion abduction and adduction there is and whether the swimmer can fully extend the fingers. The ability to change the pitch of the hand will create lift or thrust during arm movements in swimming. The smallest vortex shows that propulsion from sculling is to be anticipated. This observation of the upper limb girdle flexibility, strength and relaxation should indicate to the teacher how to achieve the optimum use of the arms in swimming. The lower limb girdle should be observed in a similar way.

Some swimmers can achieve a greater range of movement in the hip when the body is supported by the water and may even be able to 'walk' in the water, whilst not being able to do so on land. In assessing the hip joint one should ask whether the legs can be moved forwards, backwards, sideways and in what range; is the rotation in the hip joint? It should be noted whether the knee joint can be bent and stretched when under the water and, to assess the ankle joint, whether the foot can trace a circle. Can the foot be stretched and bent. The teacher should observe how movement in one joint may affect that in another joint of the same limb. This assessment of the movement in the lower limb will determine how far the legs can be used to help balance the body and if they can add to the propulsive power of the stroke.

BUOYANCY

All human bodies react in water in the same way-the heavier parts tend to sink lower than the lighter parts. Buoyancy enables the body to float, whilst 'up-thrust' in the force the water applies to a body. The composition of the body, the proportion and distribution of bone, muscle and fat are the factors which determine a person's ability to float. The teacher must make certain observations, and ask, does the person:

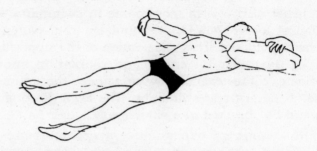

1. Float easily and very high in the water?

2. Become so tense through fear that a floating position is difficult to obtain?

3. Float in a vertical position with low legs but with the head above the water?

4. Find it difficult to float?

Teaching Strokes

The factors governing an efficient stroke are minimal resistance and maximum propulsion, and these should be the swimmer's aim.

Body Position

It is important that the position of the body in the water should be as streamlined as possible, bearing in mind that in some instances, it is not natural or comfortable for this to be achieved. Some paraplegics find that whilst supine their legs float very high, yet whilst prone their hips float high but their legs tend to drift lower in the water.

Hemiplegics may prefer to swim on the side or move vertically. If breath control is a problem, swimming on the front can be difficult; a pupil may choose to swim on the back, for example, but roll on to the front to recover to a standing position. A bobbing head action in a stroke like breast-stroke is sometimes accompanied by a steeply inclined body position.

As the confidence of the swimmer grows and as that person swims faster the body position will flatten and streamlining will be improved.

Leg Actions

For many people a leg kick is not possible, and for others adaptations have to be made. When a swimmer is likely to experience difficulties with balance, particularly as a result of having no arms or being unable to move thee arms, a symmetrical leg kick particularly whilst supine will create less of a rolling action. That person might prefer initially to be supine as the lack of arm movement would make a lifting movement of the head for breathing difficult.

Arm Actions

The arm action in conventional strokes is usually the main source of propulsion, so if there is severe physically impairment the arm movement may need to be modified; a good sculling movement can be a great asset in this situation. Symmetrical movements are often the easiest to co-ordinate and a breast-stroke arm action is frequently adapted to provide support as well as propulsion. A pull using more downward pressure is often best and, although not so proficient technically, is a useful adaptation. Balance can be difficult if there is little or no leg kick, so lifting an arm for an out of water recovery in front or back crawl may cause sinking and rotation, and therefore an underwater arm recovery may prove more successful.

Balance is often aided by a sculling type movement before recovering the arm over the water to balance the body's own lateral swing.

Breathing

Breathing should interfere as little as possible with the stroke rhythm and a rhythmical breathing pattern should be developed. The timing and type of breathing should be developed to fit the needs of the pupil and the chosen stroke.

Rhythm

A good stroke rhythm should come about through the practice of an efficient technique. The difficulty for a physically handicapped swimmer is likely to arise where there is no leg kick to balance an arm action or where the pupil is uneven or severely restricted in movement. Pupils with obvious co-ordination problems due to lack of muscle control caused by brain damage find it extremely difficult to master the co-ordination of arms and legs.

A Watership Programme

This programme should aim to give balance and confidence in the water. It should not be rushed and should incorporate fun activities which help to establish skills. The pupils should be fully involved in the learning situation. They should know why they are asked to move in a particular way or why they carry out a selected practice. The teacher should ask question also, in order to draw information from the pupils, a procedure which will encourage full involvement as well as operate as a check of their understanding up to that point.

The pupil will gain confidence in the teacher through the presentation of carefully graded tasks, with time given for repetition. Skill development should be an individualised procedure, with pupils being challenged by their own needs. This can be best achieved by the teacher adopting a flexible teaching approach and setting tasks which pupils can answer at their own level and in their own way. The lesson's content must be carefully selected to provide enjoyable activities which are fun to perform and which give a sense of achievement, success and challenge. Material must be selected to suit the physical and mental ability and the age of the pupils. Some pupils, particularly those with severe physical or mental impairment will require help from a competent partner With all non-swimmers it is important to establish certain skills:

1. The ability to submerge and recover.

2. Regaining a standing position or recovery to a safe breathing and resting position.

3. Leaving the pool with minimal assistance.

4. A variety of ways of moving in water.

5. Methods of entry into the pool.

Body Position, Balance, Recovery and Rotation

Water Activities

1. With a float in each hand and with partner support if needed, 'sit up in the water', moving your legs slowly into different shapes and direction, then recover to a sitting or standing position.

2. Push and glide in a variety of body positions; a partner may be used to initiate movement where a push is not possible. Discover which position allows your body to travel through the water most easily in both prone and supine positions.

3. Recover to a safe resting position from a supine position.

4. Float in a variety of shapes, wide, thin and round and hold the achieved shape.

5. Link balance movements together, practise gliding, floating, rotating and recovering.

6. Change between prone and supine floating positions, using pendulum-type or rotating movements.

7. Recover to a safe resting position from a prone

horizontal position. This may be a standing position holding the rail, using the rail to achieve the vertical position or by rotating to a supine float.

When teaching balance activities, establish a calm atmosphere by speaking quietly but clearly. To take up a floating or gliding position the swimmer should always start with the shoulders under the water, lean slowly into the positions by stretching the arms out sideways to give balance, and move the head towards the direction of the float. The swimmer's head can rest on the submerged shoulder of the helper.

From prone float, the swimmer should lift the head up and press down with the hands then tuck the knees up to the chest and finally place the feet firmly on the bottom of the pool. From supine float, the swimmer should bring the head forward, scoop the arms forward, then tuck the knees up to the chest and finally place the feet firmly on the bottom of the pool.

Breath Control

If swimmers are to be able to survive independently in water, it will be necessary for them to learn to maintain a rhythmic breathing pattern whilst moving through the water. This should be encouraged from the first introduction to water, or even at home in the bath or at the washbasin, when blowing bubbles can be taught. Regular breathing is necessary if an activity is to be maintained for any length of time, and it also assists relaxation in the water. The teacher should always encourage an exhalation 'blow out' as the mouth goes near the water, inhalation following automatically.

SCULLING

Sculling is a most important skill to develop. It is an arm and hand action used to balance, propel and control the body. Once a good sculling action is established, a swimmer can travel and turn in the water or use the action to balance horizontally or vertically. It can be a very strong and powerful action and even for swimmers with little movement or strength in their arms it can still be performed effectively. This involves the arms moving away from and then towards the centre line of the body.

On the outward sweep the palm is angled to face outward little finger uppermost to lead the action. On the inward sweep the thumb leads and the palm faces inwards. The sculling action should be smooth and continuous, but the speed can be varied. This action may be described as a figure of eight movement in the water. The actual position of the arms will vary according to the buoyancy of the swimmer and the shape of the body. Normally the arms should be kept close to the body with a fairly small sideways range of movement.

TEACHING SIDE STROKE

1. The arm action may be introduced by the swimmer standing in water of chest depth, bending sideways and following the action of the teacher.

2. Establish a push and glide on the side with one arm extended forward, one by the side. Check the head position.

3. Co-ordinate the stroke using key words such as pull-and-push-glide or pull-push-kick-glide. Spacing of the key words when teaching emphasises the desired rhythm.

4. Isolate the leg action if necessary. This can be taught with the legs close to the pool wall, the body in a vertical position and one side of the body close to the wall to permit the forward and backward scissor action of the legs.

5. A float can be held by the swimmer's extended arm to allow concentration on the leg action and particularly on the use of the feet.

Inverted Breast Stroke Leg Action

This stroke gives good propulsion without using any arm action, but can be further developed using a variety of arm actions.

Body Position

The body position is inclined slightly, with the head raised, to allow the hips to sink in the water, which is necessary to permit the underwater leg action.

Leg Action

From the back glide position the thighs are kept parallel with the surface of the water, the knees are opened slightly sideways and the feet lowered until they are below the knees with the feet turned out. The inside of the lower legs and feet drive out and round against the water to give propulsion, ending with the knees and feet close together.

Arm Action

The arm actions involved are a sculling action, and a larger sweeping action in which the hand and forearm push from the shoulders down the side of the body. A full double-arm action may also be used. The stroke starts in a back glide position, with the arms extended above the head, the palms facing upwards just beneath the water surface.

From the glide the arms take a pull/push actions ending at the thighs. The recovery may be over the water or returning to the glide position by drawing the arms under the water. The co-ordination is arms-legs-glide. The legs kick as the arms recover and they remain in the streamline position as the arms take their propulsive phase. This can be a very relaxed and leisurely stroke but can be developed to be quite powerful. Breathing should be regular and fitted in at the same phase of each stroke, exhalation occurring towards the end of the arm propulsion, and inhalation taking place during the arm recovery.

DOG PADDLE

The dog paddle is a valuable stage in the learning of front crawl but it also gives an easy means of travelling on the front where an out of the water arm recovery is not possible. It can be swum with the head out of the water for easy breathing, or with the head partly in the water using either forward or sideways breathing. Sometimes the arm action takes place in front of the shoulder line, but in extended dog paddle the arms should perform a full underwater pull/push action as in front crawl, pushing right through to the thighs. The arm is recovered under water, with an action similar to that in breast-stroke.

The leg action is normally a front crawl leg kick, but the stroke may be swum without a leg action or with a dolphin-type action.

Following important swimming strokes are used in modern days throughout the world :

FRONTCRAWL

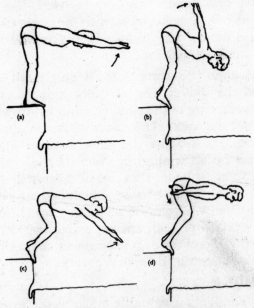

Freestyle is precisely what its name implies, namely a stroke that may be swum as the performer wishes, but it must be remembered that other countries have stricter interpretations than exist in Great Britain. Frontcrawl is a more accurate name than freestyle is a more accurate name than freestyle for the stroke that is the fastest of all.

Its characteristics are that the swimmer is on the front and rolling. The legs are under the water, kicking up and down alternately with the toes pointed, and the arms also work alternately under the water, but recover through the air. The swimmer's face is in the water, turning to the side for breathing, a movement neatly fitted into the action of the arms.

In describing a stroke in general terms, or for an individual performer, it is customary to follow a pattern:

1. Timing
2. Leg action
3. Breathing
4. Body position
5. Arm action

Timing is a description of the way in which the other four items are integrated into a complete stroke. It should be observed that some experienced teachers and coaches prefer to have arm action second, because source, and to usually the main propulsive source, and to place the leg kick third. Whichever system is adopted, the process is called analysis and is a quick, convenient method of setting down a stroke.

Leg action is traditionally second, as it is a function of the leg kick to hold the body in a good swimming position, as well as to provide some propulsion.

Breathing comes third, because distance swimming and speed swimming, apart from comfort, will not develop until an economical breathing technique, which does not interfere with the stroke, has been acquired.

Body position is placed fourth, because if the body is not in the most favourable swimming position for the individual then it must be adjusted before all else.

Arm action is fifth, as the arms are the main source of propulsion, except in most cases of breaststroke swimming, but the arms cannot work properly until the body is maintained in a swimming position by an effective leg kick.

Basic Technique and Style

Technique is the application of basic principles of swimming, which are universal, because all over the world people swim best with their bodies in a streamlined position and by pushing their hands towards their feet, for example. Style is an individual's personal interpretation of technique, so that two people could each have immaculate technique, with widely diverging styles.

Timing

Timing, often called co-ordinatiuon describes how the arm and leg actions are related to each other and to the breathing action used. The usual co-ordination in a stroke cycle is six leg kicks to one arm cycle, aptly described as 'the classic six beat style'. One arm cycle is a complete action for each of the two arms, and six divided by two equals three, so that the working arm is balanced by the opposite leg, just as i walking or running. The six beat is seen usually with an efficient kick and with a high elbow recovery. Another common co-ordination is the two beat, where there are two leg kicks to the arm cycle. It is associated with longer distances, so that one swimmer might well use six beat for sprinting, say over 50 metres, and two beat for a long swim, 400 metres for example, but in the finish of the longer race, could return to six beat.

Leg Action

All the crawl type kicks begin at the hip; frontcrawl, backcrawl and butterfly. Once the large muscles of the hip have initiated the kicking action, the lighter but sill strong muscles of the leg continue it, so that the slow movement commenced at the hip is translated into an accelerating whip of the foot.

Kicking Action

The kicking action is largely an up and down movement, up and down relative to the swimmer's own body, for it mist be remembered that the body is rolling up to 70 degrees, at which angle a large part of the kick will be in a sideways direction. Those people with loose ankles and soft feet have an advantage, and many of them quite naturally employ in-toeing, where the leg is rotated inwardly so that the big toe points inwards. This makes the foot a more efficient flipper. During the continuous kicking action, the feet pass close together, and in-toeing often places one above the other. This is a movement natural to many swimmers, who can cover long distance at good pace using their legs only for propulsion. The primary aim of the strong leg action is not propulsion, but to hold the hips, up maintaining a desirable body position for successful swimming. Variations in the kinds of kick will be dealt with later, but weak leg kicks derive from infringements of basic requirements.

Breathing

Breathing is defined as moving air out of and into the lungs. In swimming, it should interfere not at all or as little as possible with the stroke. Most physically exercise involves timing the breathing with the action and the heavier the strain, usually, the louder the grunts, as the breath is first held, then released under pressure from the build-up in the lungs and from the powerfully contracting muscles. Frontcrawl employs the very mobile shoulder joint, with its powerful muscles situated on the chest and back. The face is in the water, for periods between breaths, which causes a pressure built-up in the lungs as carbon dioxide is returned from the working tissues.

The muscles of the chest are working to move the arms, so the best time to breathe is when one arm is at entry, or catch, about to start its action and the other is recovering. This is the non-propulsive phase and is also the time of maximum acceleration when, in any stroke, it is the ideal moment to breathe. One arm is forward, waiting to start its work, and the other is recovering.

The swimmer relaxed the muscles restricting breathing, so that air leaks from the nose and mouth. Some teachers and coaches of bubbles seen from a pin-hole puncture when an air-bed or an inner tube is placed in water is considered, then obviously the leakage is but a very small part of the total. The head is turned to the chosen side and the mouth opened wide, so that the air is expelled forcefully.

If forceful breathing is performed on dry land, the contents of the abdomen can be felt pushing against the diaphragm, the main respiratory muscles. This breathing action is called 'explosive', an apt term to convey the speed with which up to five litres of air are driven out and then five litres more taken in. Although the head is turned to the side at the time of expiration and inspiration, it is often below the general level of the water, because the speed of swimming generates a wave immediately in front of the swimmer's head with a trough behind it, conveniently placed for breathing. It is a skilled action and takes time to develop. Once breathing is completed, the head is rotated so that the face is back in the water, and meanwhile the legs have continued kicking and the arms have moved on in their actions. Nothing stops, and the explosive breathing of a well trained swimmer is measured in tenths of a second.

Body Position

The frontcrawl swimmer's body position is flat and streamlined. Viewed from the side, the body does remain straight and streamlined, as it does when seen from directly above. From a head-on viewing, however, it can be seen at once that there is considerable rolling, well controlled by skilled performers. Breathing is frontcrawl involves turning the head to the side, so that streamlining is maintained as the breath is taken. Body roll aids the turning movement of the head.

The arm action of the stroke is one with recovery over the water and rolling of the body lifts the recovering shoulder and arm, which eases the recovery movement, particularly for those people who are stiff in the shoulders. The degree of roll will therefore reflect the physical characteristics of an individual, for a muscular, short necked, stiff shouldered person will roll up to 70 degrees or more in order to breath and to recover the arms comfortably and efficiently.

Head Position

The majority of swimmers adjust the head position so that the water line is cut by the forehead, but it can be cut by the eyebrows, or by the crown of the head.

Hips

Stable hips is a phrase meaning that the hips remain high and in the same relative position, so that hip stability is a sign of sound swimming. The opposite is true as well, because when control of the hips is lost, they start to sink, which means that the swimming position is also lost and resistance increases rapidly. It takes only a moment to look at a very good exponent of frontcrawl to see the apparent 'dry triangle' formed by the shoulders as the base and the two longer sides running down to the point where the spine joins the pelvis. The hips also roll at the same time as the shoulders, though usually slightly less, due to the flexibility of the spine. Those swimmers who lack flexibility will obviously roll more.

Arm Action

Arm action is sub-divided into distinct parts, though it is performed as a continuous skilled movement.

Entry

Entry is the point where the hand is placed in the water, which is somewhere between the swimmer's centre line and the shoulder line. It should not be wide of the shoulder line, not across the centre line. A moment's reflection on the streamlined position of a diver's arms will show that an entry position one, or close, to the centre line is desirable.

Pull

The pull phase of arm action develops from the catch point, as the hand accelerates due to the bending of the elbow and the arm pressing downwards, moved by the powerful muscles around the shoulder. It will be recalled that some people swim with long levers, or long arms, but that even so, there will be some elbow flexion. The very best frontcrawlers bend the elbow up to 90 degrees, but whatever degree of bending is utilised, it is at a maximum when the hand, elbow and shoulder are level. Should the elbow be leading at this point, then a weaker action is the result.

The elbow should be high, and all through the pull phase, the hand is said to be catching the elbow. Throughout this phase, good swimmers will have changed the pitch of their hands, as well as their accelerations, to attain thrust from Bernoulli principles. The hand passes underneath the face.

Push

The push phase is the final underwater movement, as the elbow is straightened powerfully and the angle of the wrist is continuously adjusted so that the palm of the hand faces backwards as much as possible. The acceleration of the hand takes it to its maximum underwater speed and its pitch is also altered. Much of the push phase is underneath the body, but finally the hand moves outwards in order to clear the hips. During the push phase, the arm is attaining a more streamlined position close to the body and as the very best frontcrawlers have the best push phases, unlike weak swimmers who fail to push right through, if they push at all, it is not difficult to conclude that **this is** the most important phase for speed.

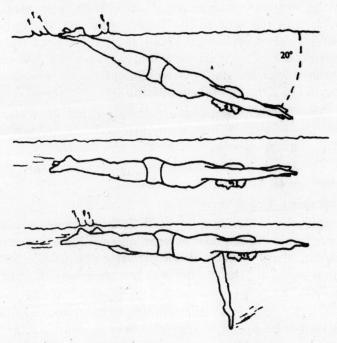

Catch

Catch is the point at which the hand begins to exert pressure on the water and this could be as early as possible, usually about eight inches or twenty centimetres below the surface. A teacher or coach checking a pulil's progress will ensure that the elbow is still higher than the hand and that the hand is shaped to press on the water. The arm is extended but not straight or stiff.

Frontcrawl Pre-requisites

1. The ability to regain the feet from the horizontal prone position. Important for small children whose

chins just clear the water.

2. The ability to open the eyes under water.

3. The possession of watermanship, which is the ability of the swimmer to be aware of his position in the water, even with his face in the water, when the eyes and ears are shut off, and to retain this ability even when some fatigue sets in, or when water unexpectedly washes over the head. Good teachers will play lots of games to ensure watermanship.

4. The ability of aquatic breathing, which is to place the head in the water, then turn or lift it to breathe and, without pause, replace it in the water.

5. The ability to kick efficiently using a float, with the head up or with the face in the water.

Teaching Frontcrawl

As in nearly all swimming, begin at the rail and transfer the exercise to the float as soon as possible to give the feeling of movement. Work through dog-paddle and stick to it until the learner has the pre-requisite listed earlier.

1. On the float. Practice breathing to the favoured side until widths are achieved with easy, continuous arm action.

2. At the rail: kicking, face down. Lift one arm, whichever is favourite, and turn the head to that side to breath. If this is too difficult, perform the action standing in water, knees bent to have shoulders under water. Establish the natural breathing sides by trial. Transfer this to the float.

3. At the rail: kicking face down; life one hand off the rail and perform one complete arm action while breathing to that side. The hand must be placed back on the rail after breathing is over. Transfer this to the float. Stress that the hand on the breathing side must be replaced on the float after the breath has been

taken.

4. Full Stroke:

1. Swim widths with two breaths, then **three**.

2. Swim widths without breathing.

3. Swim widths with one breath, taken half-way across.

4. Build a continuous swim across the width with breaths taken every stroke to the natural side.

BUTTERFLY

Butterfly is a powerful and handsome stroke when swum by a well-prepared swimmer, but many swimmers, teachers and coaches are shy of it because it appears to be demanding, both of the swimmer and of the instructor.

Breaststroke butterfly combined a breaststroke leg kick with a double crawl arm action, and the legs and arms worked alternately, sometimes with a slight glide. It is not seen in competition at higher levels, though it remains a useful progression to dolphin butterfly for natural breaststroke swimmers and is a fun swim for short distances. It is governed by swimming laws which require the performer to:

1. Kick the legs simultaneously in a vertical plane.

2. Swim on the front with shoulders square.

3. Recover the arms simultaneously and symmetrically over the water.

4. Swim on the front with the shoulders horizontal.

5. Use the arms simultaneously and symmetrically under the water.

Leg Action

In all strokes it is difficult to isolate one section, and this is particularly true to butterfly, where the body, legs, arms and breathing are closely integrated in their movements. Swimming laws require the legs to kick up and down side by side, which they do in compensation for the upper body and arm movements.

The double leg kick is initiated by the very powerful hip muscles, so that the tops of the feet and the legs press on the water partly downward and partly backwards. The backward component gives a forward reaction for propulsion, but the downward component lifts the upper body which is sinking due to arm recovery, with or without the head movement for breathing. From their deepest point, the feet move up as the knees are bent and the hips sink.

There is discussion as to whether this upward movement of the sole of the foot gives propulsion, in the butterfly or the frontcrawl and, similarly, in the downward movement in backcrawl. Should there be propulsion, it would be a small fraction of the reaction produced by the powerful hip and knee extension. Many skilled swimmers finish the down kick with inward rotation of the legs, producing the desirable in-toeing position.

Checkpoints

The leg action must be:

1. From the hip
2. Continues
3. Simultaneous
4. Effective.

If the hips lose stability, allowing the body position to deteriorate, then the kick is ineffective.

Breathing

Breathing is of the explosive type, with leakage of air from the nose and mouth starting underwater as the lungs fill and the muscles around the chest work powerfully on the arms. As the mouth clears the water, the neck is extended the lungs are explosively emptied are immediately refilled. At this point the arms are completing or have completed, the push or phase, which is also the point of maximum acceleration in the stroke cycle. The mouth closes and the head is speedily returned to its normal swimming position, before the arms complete their recovery.

The whole breathing movement takes a few tenths of a second and needs powerful muscles of respirations. The mouth is facing directly forward and teachers and coaches should watch to see that learners, or more experienced swimmers in a demanding session, do not turn the head to one side.

Body Position

The body rises and falls in a movement which is often greater on the breathing stroke, but the centres of gravity and buoyancy are given minimum displacement. It may be likened to a well-sprung car moving over a very bumpy road. The head, on the non-breathing stroke, is held centrally with the face in the water and the water-level cutting the crown, very similar to its frontcrawl position, but often deeper. Because the head is somewhat lower while the breath is held, the shoulders are that much relatively higher than in frontcrawl and, because the stroke is swum on the breast, without body roll, a slightly humpbacked position may be seen at certain points in the stroke cycle. Hips rise, until the seat is close to the surface.

Those who overstress the movement may have the seat clearly out of the water. At the lowest point, the hips will sink to just beyond the body's own depth. Hip flexibility is needed and 'disco dancing' while standing in shoulder depth water is an interesting introduction to butterfly for those without natural feel for the undulation required. Flexion of the knees is up to 90 degrees, the greatest angle of the crawl type leg actions and with this degree of bend, parts of the feet may break the surface. During the breathing stroke, the head and shoulders rise until the chin is pushed forwards by extending the neck.

The hips will sink lower and in this position, though the same degree of knee bend is made, the feet may not break the surface.

Timing

There are some strong swimmers who have a long push in the arm action and that conversely there are those who have a weak incomplete push, or no push at all. If the swimmer has a strong push phase, then the feet and hips will react but, obviously, a weak push evokes a weak reaction and the absence of a push will produce no reaction at all. Experienced observers of swimmers will recognise the similar body adjustment and foot movement present in a breaststroke start or turn due to the long push through of the hands permitted at that time. Therefore, in butterfly of good technique, there are two legs kicks to one arm cycle.

The first leg kick is to counterbalance the down thrust of the overwater arm recovery, coupled with the down thrust of the head and shoulders on the breathing stroke. This first kick occurs as the head is returned to the water, swiftly followed by the arms. The second leg kick, if present, occurs at thee end of a strong push phase or, should there be an incomplete push, when the hands cease to exert pressure. A descriptive helpful teaching and coaching points is 'kick the hands in and kick the hand out'. Many proficient swimmers have the two kicks of similar strength, in which case they are termed equal beat. When the second kick is obviously weaker than the first, it is called a major minor kick. Absence of any second kick leads logically to the single beat.

Arm Action

Pull Phase

The hands press out, but are still moving backwards and downwards in a movement sometimes inaptly described as a double frontcrawl arm action, because it resembles more a breaststroke arm pull, when viewed from ahead, or from the side. During the accelerating movement, the hands change pitch so that at the completion of the pull phase, the palms are facing back and the hands, elbows and shoulders are all in line, an excellent position for a powerful push. Some swimmers will have their hands wider of the elbows than others, which reflects personal physical build.

Entry

A diver hold the arms in a streamlined position to minimise resistance, and similarly a swimmer in frontcrawl and backcrawl, may enter one hand at the most advantageous point, the centre line. Some exceptionally flexible butterfly swimmers of high buoyancy and power are able to enter the hands close to the centre line, but usually the entry will be on the shoulder line, or inside it.

An entry outside the shoulder line gives poor streamlining and is to be avoided. The hands usually have a long entry, as the arms are long, but not rigged. Some swimmers have a short underwater extension of the hands and arms as seen in frontcrawl. Normally the hands are entered pitched, with the thumbs down and the palms facing part downward and part outward. Shoulder flexibility will be an important factor in deciding the entry position, but whichever entry point is selected the elbow must be higher than the hand.

Push Phase

There is no pause, but the hands push backwards and also move closer together, under the body, in an accelerating movement accompanied by a change of pitch in the hands. The distance between thee hands as they push back is again a reflection of the performer's physical built, and it may be close enough for the thumbs nearly to touch, or almost the width of the body apart. The push must, however, be under the body and it continues to accelerate. When the arms are nearly straight, with the hands angled to face backwards, they swing out to clear the hips in preparation for release and recovery, after reaching maximum speed.

Catch

Catch point, as in all skilled swimming, should be early. Less buoyant butterfly swimmers have a larger downward component to raise the upper body, but the hands also press out and back, with the elbow high. Beginners and tiring learners drop the elbow, so it will lead into a weak arm action.

Recovery

Following the final acceleration in the push, the elbows flex to lift part of the arm clear of the water, as the arm rotates so that the hand slices out of the water, little finger up, although some swimmers hold the hands palm up in a continuation of the push, and some have the thumb a little higher. From here the arms swing in a fast, relaxed, circular movement, clearing the water. Swimmers fortunate in their buoyancy and flexibility, may keep the hands palm down, but a sound, practical teaching and coaching point is to have the hands with the little finger up, or even with the palms facing slightly up. With the arm in this position, the elbow is high and the shoulder joint unlocked, allowing maximum clearance over the water. Further, holding the hands at this angle, is a continuation of the palm or thumb uppermost release described earlier and a preparation for the pitched, soft entry, elbow high. Some swimmers fling the arms forward in recovery using much speed and strength.

Centripetal force will then straighten the arms, although an acceptable entry is still obtainable. This high speed recovery is sometimes seen in learners and in those with poor buoyancy and shoulder mobility, because for them it is urgent to get their arms forward and into the water as early as possible. The arms provide the main propulsion is butterfly.

Butterfly Pre-requisites

1. The ability to open the eyes underwater.

2. Watermanship of a high order.

3. Aquatic breathing.

4. A developed front and backcrawl kick.

5. The ability to swim in straight lines.

6. A streamlined push and glide from the wall.

Teaching Butterfly

It has long been assured that butterfly should be taught last of the four recognised strokes, but some swimming teachers have discovered that the stroke can be introduced as fun to young beginners. It is possible for children to enjoy short distances swimming their version of the butterfly, provided that the teacher uses common sense and keeps the demand low. Begin at the rail, with a double leg kick. 'Feet tied together' is a teaching point children grasp readily.

Transfer the leg kick to a float, with the child on the front or on the back. The latter is another way of reducing the demand on a learner and progresses to the same action without a supporting float, but with sculling. A parallel progression is the dolphin leg kick with breaststroke arm action, which neatly co-ordinates with a quick lift of the head for breathing. Children also enjoy trying to swim on the side underwater imitating a fish. The arm action is taught with the child in shallow water shoulders under, performing the double, circular arm action, which gives the feeling of the arm movement underwater and of the recovery through the air.

Make sure that the arm is long and that the action is not with elbows leading. For the next progression, it is necessary to arrange the pupil, or pupils according to height, so that the water-line is comfortably at the shoulder. The learner jumps, from both ˙feet, lifting the body a little from the water, and makes the arm action simultaneously with the jump. Following this, the learner adds ducking underwater after the jump so that the arms are down as the head is under, which simulates the feeling of butterfly. The logical progression is to move across the pool, using the double foot jump and the double arm action, at which stage some learners lean forward, which raises the feet, and swim a stroke or two of butterfly. This last progression is known as 'kangaroo jumps'. With the distances limited, the learner is able to swim short bursts without breathing while the stoke rhythm and coordination develop.

A lot of teaching and learning time must be devoted to letting the stroke grow with the use of one arm drills, when the swimmer has one hand grasping the float and the other arm is used in a butterfly action, initially with the head up, or with the body rolled to one side for ease of breathing, but later with the face in the water, lifting for a breath at the correct time. Similar one arm drills can be built around swimming on the back and eventually the front or back drills are repeated, but without a float. A very successful drill is to swim with, say, left arm only, right arm only, both arms together and with a breath. It helps learners cosiderably if momentum into the stroke is gained from a vigorous push off the wall or from a plunge dive, when the arm and leg action match the speed of the streamlined body.

BACKCRAWL

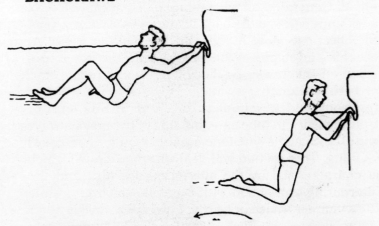

Any stroke swum on the back is a form of backstroke, of which backcrawl is one. Old English backstroke uses a breaststroke type leg kick, with a double arm action involving an overwater recovery, though it can be swum with the arms recovering at the side of the body and in the water, for part of their return. Life-saving leg kick uses a breaststroke type leg action as well, and the hands may scull at the sides of the body, aiding propulsion, or are free for any life-saving skills. Back-paddle, or back sculling, the counter-part of front or dog-paddle, is a swimming skill in its own right, as well as an essential progression towards backcrawl. It is economical in its energy demands, once learned, and uses an alternating crawl kick, while the hands scull at the side of the hips. Backstrokes are to be considered as resting strokes, because the majority of swimmers, even powerful ones, will turn on to the back for a respite at demanding times, to have the face clear of the water.

The main disadvantage of backstroke is that the swimmer is unable to see the way ahead, unless the head is turned at an awkward and uncomfortable angle. Generally, all swimming is remarkably free of accidents, but it is the backstroke swimmers who tend to collect the most bumps, on the head or hand. At coaching level, one of the most painful knocks occurs when a backcrawler pushes off hard, in a racing start or turn, as another swimmer approaches the end of the pool. Older swimmers involved in this level of training learn to take care, but one of the tasks always with the coach is safe lane organisation for backcrawl training. This section will deal with backcrawl, which is characterised by the alternating leg kick and the alternating arm action with overwater recovery, while the swimmer is face upwards. Good backcrawl is never swum flat on the back, because the body obviously rolls. Swimming law allows the swimmer to roll up to 90 degrees each way. In other words, if the body is not on its front, then it must be on its back.

Body Position

The body assumes a shallow dish shape, which is similar to that used by good gymnasts in handstands. It is a strong position. The head is held slightly up, as though resting on a cushion, and the phrase 'head pillowed on the water' is accurate and descriptive. The actual head angle adopted by a person will depend on individual physical characteristics, as raising the head higher will cause the feet to drop, while pushing it back raises them. If the head is held out of the water, as learners are apt to do, it causes the hips to drop and an unacceptable swimming position is the result.

During backcrawl swimming, the head remains very steady, and it is this appearance which leads unquestioning observers to assume that the body has the same steadiness, when in reality good technique requires body roll. Normal limits of head position will have the nose pointing somewhere between straight up, and to an angle of approximately 45 degrees away from the vertical towards the feet. The shoulders are high and the hips are also well up to the surface but not as high as in frontcrawl.

Leg Action

Leg action has alternating flexion and extension of the knee, but the knee should not break the surface. Flexion is greater than in frontcrawl, because the foot is dropping downwards. The feet kick up to the surface, but too much splash is indicative of poor swimming and the toes should just lift to, but not break, the surface. When viewed from head-on, it is apparent that there are two extreme styles, one using a position with the line of the shoulders remaining parallel to the surface of the water, and the other with the shoulders rolling so that the degrees to the left and to the right. Between these two extremes, every possible variation can be found. The hips and feet roll with the body, so that a large component of the kick is sideways at certain moments, and not simply up and down in a vertical plane. It is to be observed that some swimmers roll the shoulders more than the hips, while others roll the body as one unit.

From head on, it can be seen that the feet react towards the working arm and thee hips away from it, so that as the right arm acts, the feet move to the right and the hips to the left. Because the arm action is of necessity further from the centre line of the body than it is in frontcrawl, the reactions are more marked. It is called lateral deviation. This deviation is most easily seen from directly above.

Good technique minimises it, but beginners may have a snaking action, sometimes made worse by moving the head from side to side. It is good teaching to tell beginners to imagine that there is a glass of milk balanced on the forehead and to try to swim without spilling it.

Breathing

It is said that breathing in backcrawl is no problem because the face is clear of the water. This takes no account of the fact that some of the muscles around the chest, front and back, also steady the shoulder joint, or are very active in the powerful, fast arm action required. If breathing takes place at the wrong time, it may well interfere with the stroke. A number of mechanically poor movements derive from a relaxation of the chest wall when it needs to be firm.

Arm Action

There are two extremes of body position, when the view is from head-on. One had the shoulder line staying generally parallel with the surface of the water, and the other with the shoulder line rolling up to 70 degrees. Mechanically, all human movement requires the use of short levers and long levers alternately.

In swimming, the great range of movement available at the shoulder, coupled with elbow flexion, makes the arms powerful, more so in frontcrawl than in backcrawl, where the latter imposes restrictions on the range of mobility. When these two facts are linked, it can be understood that keeping the shoulders relatively flat means that a long arm must be used, or the hand would protrude from the water as the elbow bends. With shoulder roll, the arm deep in the water can bend up to 90 degrees safely, ensuring a powerful flexion and extension at the elbow. It is of interest to note the range of shoulder positions adopted by swimmers. The small shoulder roll with a long arm may be likened to the pace and action of an afternoon stroll, and the large shoulder roll with a well flexed elbow to the pace and action of a track sprinter. These two extremes are referred to as long arm backcrawl and bent arm backcrawl, which is rather misleading because the same distinctions are observable in all swimming.

Catch Position

Long arm action, with little body roll, has a catch position some 6 to 8 inches below the surface with the palm facing outwards. The total movement of the arm will be a long semi-circular one, but initially it is with the palm facing outwards. For every action there is an equal opposite reaction, so lateral deviation will be marked. Bent arm action, with large body roll, has the hand facing largely downwards towards the bottom of the pool, so that skilled backcrawl swimmers exert a downward press on the water very early in the arm action, as in all strokes. It is more likely to be omitted from backcrawl than all other strokes, and teachers and coaches are heard giving the instruction to 'roll and press' in endeavours to include an early pressure in their swimmers' repertoires of skills.

Push Phase

Use of the long arm action produces little push as there is little flexion of the elbow. In this action, the arm and hand continue in a large semi-circle, with the palm facing more and more towards the swimmer's thigh, where the movement ends, having achieved insufficient acceleration and a reaction to one side. Where the deep, scooping action below the body is used, from its position at the end of the first half of the underwater movement, the hand continues in a long, slow arc to bring it alongside the high, sometimes with the palm up.

The law of action and reaction will cause the hips to move down. Employment of bent arm action places the arm and hand an ideal position at the end of the pull phase, with the elbow well flexed and the palm facing backwards. A powerful accelerating push occurs as the elbows is straightened and the arm extends close down the side of the body, where it also gives far less resistance. The final movement, as the hand changes its pitch, is a strong push towards the bottom of the pool, which aids propulsion and the rolling of the body towards the other arm. The speed and pitch of the hand allow application of Bernoulli principles, which combine with the low resistance position of the arm to give speed and economy of effort.

Entry

The point at which the hand enters the water will depend on personal characteristics and on the techniques used. Entries between the swimmer's own centre line and shoulder line are acceptable, preferably closer to the centre line, which should not be crossed.

Knowledgeable teachers and coaches make allowance for any lateral deviation before pronouncing exactly where one particular swimmer enters his hand, and they also know that one swimmer may have different entry points for each hand.

At entry, the arm is stretched but not stiff, and the shoulder is elevated as when reaching up to a shelf, but over-extension of any joint places it in a weak mechanical position and needs to be watched in advanced teaching and coaching. The hand is turned palm outwards so that the little finger enters first, with minimum splash, as the arm brushes the ear on that side of the head.

<u>Recovery</u>

The long arm action, in a shallow semi-circle ends with the palm of the hand alongside the thigh, thumb uppermost. A similar position may occur at completion of the least desirable long arm action, in a deep semi-circle, but this kind of arm action may end with the palm up, in which case rotation of the arm will bring the thumb uppermost. The bent arm action leaves the hand well below the surface, palm down, so recovery begins from this situation.

Some swimmers simply lift the arm straight up and the hand emerges with its back uppermost. Others rotate the arm outwards and lift simultaneously to bring the hand out with its thumb uppermost and palm facing inwards. A third option is to rotate the arm inwards, so the hand breaks surface with the little finger on top and the palm facing outwards. After breaking the surface, the recovery movements of the different underwater actions are similar.

The arm is lifted straight up without crossing the swimmer's body or moving to one side. Crossing the body may cascade water onto a learner's face and cause discomfort. Moving the arm away to one side leads to an entry wide of the shoulder, which is also undesirable. At some time in this movement, the arm must be rotated so that the little finger leads backwards and the palm is facing outwards. This rotation unlocks the shoulder joint and permits a full movement which would not be possible with the thumb leading and the palm facing inwards.

Hence, there are a number of reasons for recovering the arm with the palm facing outwards and the little finger leading:

1. The hand breaks the surface cleanly on release.

2. The shoulder joint is unlocked.

3. The shoulder of the recovering arm is lifted clear of the water, thus reducing resistance.

4. The hand is shaped ready for entry.

From the highest position above the shoulder, the hand accelerates to entry and to repeat its underwater propulsive action.

Timing

All backcrawlers must have an efficient leg kick. Those unable to develop such a kick turn to other strokes, so timing in backcrawl is usually very simple. There is one complete arm cycle to six leg kicks and, as in frontcrawl, two arm actions divided into six leg is always balancing the opposite arm, as in walking. A four beat kick is found, but it is rare, with its slow, deep leg movement. Should you wish to check your own or another swimmer's timing, consider either hand as it enters the water, when it should be balanced by the opposite leg with the toes just popping up.

Backcrawl Pre-requisites

1. The ability to accept water splashed on the face, as against being able to place the head in the water.

2. The ability to swim back-paddle.

3. The ability to regain the feet from a supine position.

4. The ability to be able to turn from the back onto the front and continue swimming.

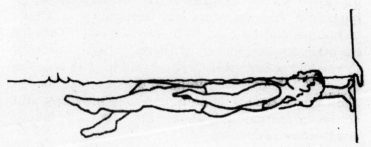

Teaching Backcrawl

Non-swimmers are able to feel what it is like to be on the back by holding on to the rail, or to the trough, raising their legs and body so that a semi-supine position is reached, and then pulling themselves along head first and having the sensation of the water flowing over the skin. It is difficult and uncomfortable to learn backcrawl at the rail or trough. Progression is made from dog-paddle to back-paddle, using buoyancy aids to hold the body safely on the back while the leg kick is attempted. To this, sculling with one or both hands can be added and, as confidence and skill increase, the buoyancy aid removed, until a true back-paddle results. The arm action can be taught with the learner walking backwards and keeping the shoulders level with the water, before it is developed with one or both arms working, from the back-paddle.

A useful method is to have the learner swim vigorously on back-paddle, sculling hard, upon a signal or word from the teacher, to attempt the full arm action for a short distance. One-arm exercises, combined with use of a buoyancy aid, are most useful, as the learner can give full attention of the technique wanted. Once the natural rhythm and technique are established, the distance swum is gradually increased, when backcrawl, because of its less demanding breathing technique, can be used to build up basic fitness for the other strokes. Remember to encourage swimmers to 'roll and press'. Every teacher will have to face the choice of teaching long arm or bent arm action. For adult learners there is nothing wrong with long arm action in recreational swimming. Slow swimming involves low resistance.

BREASTSTROKE

Breaststroke, is one of its many forms, is the life-saving stroke, because anybody unfortunate enough to fall into water unexpectedly is most unlikely to swim frontcrawl, backcrawl or butterfly to rescue themselves and, if rescuing some other person, the final approach at least should be made on breaststroke in order to have the best view of the position. Because the limbs remain below the surface, the breaststroke gives maximum flotation, but pays a penalty as the underwater recovery of the arms and legs, after their propulsive actions, causes resistance. It is a go-stop stroke, of which the mechanics were for a long time misunderstood, as it was believed that the squeezing together action of the legs produced forward propulsion. In common with other strokes, too, it was believed that a long, straight arm gave the best leverage, until teachers and coaches carefully examined what the best swimmers were doing and thought about why these techniques were successful. Swimming law has strict requirements for breaststroke.

1. Part of the head must be above the general level of the water at all times.

2. The feet must be turned outward in the characteristic position for breaststroke propulsion. It is called dorsi-flexion and the opposite movement, which points the feet and toes as in the crawl strokes, is called plantar flexion.

3. The limb movements must be under or along the surface.

4. The body must remain on the breast at all times, with the shoulders parallel to the surface of the water and square to the front.

5. The arm and leg movements respectively, must be simultaneous and symmetrical and movements of the feet up and down are not permitted.

<u>Body Position</u>

The ideal swimming position is a streamlined one, as taken up good divers. Movements of limbs away from this shape, or deviation of the whole shape, produce resistance. Breaststroke swimmers must breathe regularly, and the simplest solution is to hold the head out of the water all the time and swim with the body angled downwards to a greater or lesser degree. Recreational swimmeers and learners choose this position, as thee face is clear of the water, giving easy breathing and clear vision. The resistance factor is unimportant because these swimmers have little interest in speed.

Resistance is largely a problem which comes with speed, so the adoption of an angled body position, permanently deviating from the ideal, does not matter to recreational swimmers. It is described as swimming with a fixed head position. The ideal swimming position is also often described as being flat and streamlined. If a breaststroke tries to be flat, with the hips well up as in the frontcrawl, then the feet would break the surface, which contravenes swimming law. Should the breaststroke decide to submerge the body completely, in order to keep the feet underwater, then the head could well be underwater also, in contravention of swimming law.

Various compromises are to be seen as solutions to this dilemma. There are some swimmers who hold the head up and angle the hips of keep the feet under and, as the strong, propulsive kick is made, the lower the head into the water, carefully keeping part of its above water. For part of the stroke cycle, it allows streamlined position, which is often held as a glide, giving economically swimming. Those with high buoyancy are able to use this kind of technique, and sinkers might just have a brief glide. The movement of lowering the heads is at times exaggerated or over-vigorous and gives rise to an ungainly rocking body movement. Another solution to the dilemma has been developed by top class breaststroke swimmers and comprises swimming with the hips in a fixed position, safely below the surface so that the leg action, while a part of the head is legally showing above the surface. This creates a body position for a powerful leg, kicking directly backwards, without a large wasteful component angled downwards.

The breathing takes place with a lift of the head and shoulders, sufficient to have the mouth clear the large wave pushed up by the raised upper body. Breath must be taken very quickly and the head and shoulders lowered at once to remove the high resistance. It is a compromise and the powerful leg action is strong enough to compensate amply for the resistance. Young swimmeers and their instructors are as prone to follow new styles as people everywhere, and the raising of the head and shoulders for breathing is to be seen segregated, as is the fast return of the head and shoulders to the water, with a movement similar to one in dolphin butterfly. Teachers and coaches will wisely have their swimmers try all techniques and settle on that which best matches the individual.

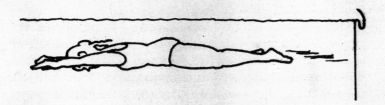

Arm Action

Most breaststroke swimmers gain the larger part of their propulsion from the leg action, although there are some whose arm and leg action contribute approximately half each, and there are a few whose physical build gives them an arm action which dominates the stroke. Swimming law requires the limb movements to be under the water, and consequently analysis of breaststroke excludes entry. There must be discussion of the arms and hands in the glide position, where they are extended forward, often with the pains down and the thumbs touching, in a steamlined position. Care must be taken to avoid excessive extension of the shoulder, which may so place the joint that the muscles action is weakened. Another arm and hand position frequently met is with the thumbs touching and with the little finger raised, so that the palms are facing both outward and downward. The inward rotation of the arm which achieves this, is analogous to the soft, pitched entry used in the other three strokes, in that the elbow is raised and thus prepared for high elbow arm action. When the palm down position described in the previous paragraph is used, the elbows are underneath the arm and liable to lead the action. Elbow leading movements are propulsively weak though suited to many learners and to recreational swimmers.

Pull Phase-Straight Arm Action

A straight arm action must involves some degree of elbow flexion and extension but it is a discreditable title, as the arms show little flexion. From the catch, the arms pull sideways and downwards, the depth of the pull depending on several factors. Beginners may well press down considerably, because reaction will lift the head and shoulders. Recreational swimmers of high buoyancy, with no difficulty in keeping the face clear of thee water, may well pull mainly sideways. The straight arm pull usually ends with each arm held at 45 degrees outwards and 45 degrees downwards from the centre line, but obviously some have a narrower or wider action to meet personal physical build. The fingertips are normally just at the edge of the field of vision, when the eyes are looking straight ahead. If the wider action is used, there are some who pull until the arms are stretched out sideways, level with or even beyond the shoulders. This is an error, even though the performer may enjoy the feeling of using strength, because the action leaves the arms in a high resistance position and one from which further resistance will be created as the arms are recovered for the next stroke. Recovery is effected by bending the elbows, while moving the hands inwards. Several common errors occur at this stage. As the hands come together, the elbows are held in a fixed position, which gives high resistance.

If the hands are slid palms downwards towards each other until the thumbs tough, it adds to the tendency to hold the elbows out. It helps if the palms face each other, or at least face partly inwards, as this streamlines the elbow position. Some learners are taught, by word and by demonstration, to recover the hands in the position close under the chin. The action, for a person in a prone position in water and not standing upright on the poolside, is actually deeper, at approximately the same depth as the elbows, or a little above them. From this point, the hands are pushed forward until ready to start the sequence again.

Pull Phase-Bent Arm Action

The hands are pressed downwards, sideways and backwards, initially with the palms facing partly outwards, but changing pitch through the movement until they are facing backwards. Flexion of the elbow is kept high. It is an accelerating movement, reaching a position where the elbows are wide of the shoulders, below them. The hands are usually wide of the elbows, but some swimmers have them at the same width or inside it, in order to shorten the lever. The effective length of the lever is a line from the pivot point in the shoulder to the hands. The arm pull should end when level with the shoulders, as stated above, the there can be no push phase in the sense of the long push through used in the other three strokes.

However, some experienced teachers and coaches argue that the next movement is a push and describe it as such. During the last stages of the pull and as a smooth, accelerating continuation of it, the elbows begin to bend and the hands move rapidly together. As they do so, the hands change pitch so that from facing backwards, fingertips down, they end with the palms facing each other, fingertips pointing forward.

The movement is aptly describe as a swirl, and it is a powerful sculling action, the speed of which combines with the hand's pitch changes to use Bernoulli principles to gain thrust. Some swimmers continue the pitch changing the hands by rotating the arms outwards until the palms are facing partly or directly upwards. Such rotation may be classed as one of the exaggerated movements mentioned several times earlier, but it has the beneficial effect of streamlining the elbows, in an action described as 'shunting the elbows'.

Catch Point

In the other three recognised strokes, the catch is some few inches below the surface, usually six to eight inches. In these strokes, following entry, the hand or hands move immediately to catch point. In breaststroke, many swimmeers are taught to push the hands forward, just below the surface, where they are frequently held in a glide action. Close observation shows that swimmers may have a shorter or longer arm glide coupled with a leg glide, but there are those who have an arm glide and no leg slide. The opposite is also to be found. If the hands are pushed forward together in a shallow action, with or without a subsequent glide, there is a delayed downward and outward movement to catch point.

A coaching instruction to swimmers sometimes heard, is for the hands to be pushed forward and, as the arms extend, for the hands then to be pushed downward in an action reminiscent of the early press upon the water found in good crawl and butterfly swimming. It avoids the brief delay. Swimmers using the palm downward starting position tend to drift the hands apart and downward which is acceptable for leisurely swimming. Competitive swimmers need the early catch point, with the hands and arms shaped for the succeeding pull phase.

Leg Action

There are two distinct leg actions, and study of old printed and photographic material relevant to breaststroke shows that during the period when one action was being exclusively taught, the second and better kick was used by swimmers to whom it came quite naturally.

The Wedge

The wedge kick has been taught for many years, and was based on spreading the legs and squeezing away the wedge of water they held between them, by closing the gap. Trials with straight legs, while ensuring that there is no ankle movement, show this to be impossible for movement derives from bending and straightening a limb. It also puts the legs in a position of great resistance. This having been stated, it must be recognised that there are swimmers who, for a number of physical reasons, are happy with the wedge kick, which is sufficient for recreation. Seen from the side, the legs are recovered from the stretched glide position, being brought forwards and flexed until there is either a right angle at the hip, with the thighs pointing straight down, knees flexed, or with the knees brought further forward of this position, so that the thighs are pointing forward and downward. It is a high resistance position and the further forward the knees are carried, the higher the drag. In breaststroke the leg is the lever, and it is the inside of the foot which becomes the paddle when dorsi-flexed.

The recovered position described in the previous paragraph places the foot so that at worst the sole is facing backwards and at best, partly backwares, which gives the instep an impossible or poor position for thrust. From this position the legs are straightened, often as wide as possible, the actual angle depending on personal hip mobility. The soles of the feet press on the water, or only part of the instep presses, usually late in the leg extension. Resistance comes from the wide spread of the legs, and it decreases as the legs close to hip width or inside it. This is referred to as being inside the body's shadow or shilhouette, which implies a low resistance. It is late in the leg action when there is sufficient propulsion to overcome the high resistance. Viewed from the rear, the recovered position shows that often the heels are touching and that the knees are spread much wider than the width of the hips.

The soles of the feet face backwards, or partly so, depending on the knee and hip relationship. As the legs extend, they straighten while remaining outside the width of the hips, which leaves no further contribution to be made to propulsion but an addition to resistance instead. The legs squeeze together and the heels touch with the toes pointed, many swimmers having been taught to complete the leg action by bringing the heels together. There is small acceleration of the feet during the wedge kick.

The Whip Kick

The whip kick is mechanically more efficient than the wedge. Viewed from the side, the knees are well behind a vertical line descending from the hip, which gives a smoother water flow, lessening the resistance. The inside surface of the foot faces backward, where it can gain maximum purchase on the water, the equivalent of a good catch point for the hands. This comparison with the hands is one which is very descriptive of outstanding breaststroke, who appear to possess in the feet a feel and sensitivity normally associated with supple hands.

From the recovered position, the legs extend backwards and there is often a weak downward component. When viewed from the rear, the recovered positions of whip kick breaststroke show a range of attitudes deriving from individual characteristics. The teacher or coach will look at the distance between the heels and between the knees. When seen like this and associated with the individual hip width of the swimmer, the three widths, feet, hips, knees, may be generated as a capital W. The 'breaststroke W', as it is called, varies considerably, some being tall and narrow and other being wider, either at the top or the bottom. From the W position adopted, the legs kick back in an accelerating movement, the heels leading in a patch which moves out and then in, thus creating a curved limb track, better seen from directly overhead. The radios of the curve will depend on the individual physical build of the swimmer but the end result is that the legs straighten only when behind the hips, inside the body shadow, so that propulsion is gained all the way and resistance minimised. The accelerating movement is often continued by expert, natural swimmers, so that it ends with the big toes touching due to strong inward rotation of the legs, combining with the speed attained to give a propeller action as the feet change from a dorst-flexed position to an extended streamlined one. The swirl of the feet in this action strongly reminiscent of the pitching of the hands in sculling.

Breathing

For the leisure swimmer, breathing brings no difficulty, as the face is clear of the water, or a small movement makes it so. Those swimming with a fixed head position and learners, will almost certainly breathe when the arms are extended forward, or moving forward to that position. Often the breath is taken at the same time as a glide, whether a full glide or a partial one. The slow long arm action lends itself to slow breathing, and the lungs empty and refill with an easy trickling in and out of air. Bubbles show that air is leaking from the mouth underwater, but the great part of exhalation happens with the mouth above water, to be followed at once by inhalation. Breath is taken once every stroke cycle. The bent arm action, with a whip kick, used by competitive swimmers, employs fast movements of the limbs and the head is partly submerged with the fixed hip body position.

Raising the head and shoulders at racing speeds raises a large wave directly in front of the swimmer. In consequence of these factors, explosive breathing is used. Some air is exhaled underwater, but the powerful exhalation is largely completed as the chin is pushed forward and the mouth is clear of the water. On the rebound of the powerful use of respiratory muscles, inhalation occurs, and the head and shoulders return quickly to a more streamlined position. Most competitive swimmers breathe every stroke cycle, although breath holding to retain a streamlined position might be used at the end of a race with a close finish.

Timing

The long arm breaststroke swimmer takes breath at the non-propulsive stage of the stroke cycle and also at the point of maximum acceleration. Leg action is the main propulsive force in breaststroke, and the body moves forward as the legs finish their kick, at which time the arms are being extended forward. Exhalation takes place at this time and is called early breathing. Many thousands of children have been taught with the instruction to 'blow their fingers forward,' which leads at once to early breathing. Slight variations exist as the precise moment breathing, but the arms are well forward. The timing fits to the rhythm of arm pull; leg kick; breathe: arm pull; leg kick; breathe. Or arm pull; leg kick, breathe and glide and repeat. It can be thought of as 'breathing off the legs', a descriptive phrase. Bent arm breaststroke, with its who kick and explosive breathing, has a radically different timing, but it obeys the rules of breathing at a non-propulsive stage and when the body has its highest speed.

Directly thee arms and hands have completed the swirling action, the head and shoulders are raised for the breath and then returned to the water, as the powerful whip kick is executed and the arms are extended forward. The rhythm of the timing is: pull; breathe: kick; pull; breath; kick. Sometimes there is a slight pause following the arm pull and the rhythm could be written: pull; breathe .....; kick pull; breathe......kick. Because of the vast range of build, age, strength and flexibility found among swimmers, there will exist a parallel range of timings, with those above as the extremes.

One example is termed 'mid-way breathing' in breaststroke, and needs little explanation, beyond saying that the arms are half-way through the pull action. In an earlier section, attention was drawn to the necessity of breath holding during physical exercise. No breath should be taken until the arms have completed their movements, because the muscles moving the arms are grouped around the chest wall, so that the relaxation of the chest wall concomitant with breathing reduces the effectiveness of the arm action, even to the point of stopping it completely. It follows that, normally, breathing is best left until the arms have finished their task, but in breaststroke it is possible to breathe at any point in the arm action. The teacher will notice that those swimmers with stronger arms will pull perhaps a third, a half, or two-thirds of the way through the possible full arm movement and then take breath. Also, the teacher will notice some swimmers with weaker arms who use just a small hand movement and then take breath, so that they are virtually swimming with the legs only.

Breaststroke Pre-requisites

There are none. The most important decision is to use the multi-stroke methods of teaching and watch for those who are natural breaststrokers.

Teaching Breastroke

Human beings can be grouped in many ways: some are tall and some are short: some are thin and some are fat: there are women and there are men. They also are found to be naturally symmetrical or naturally alternating in limb movements, and therefore take naturally to breaststroke, or otherwise. In the crawl type strokes, the water pressure is sensed by the nerve endings present on the top of the foot. Breaststroke, with its dorsi-flexed foot position, requires that the water pressure is sensed by nerve endings situated on the inner surfaces of the foot. Once a swimmer has found how to gain propulsion, with either the top of the foot, or with its inside surface, there is often impedance to learning the other one.

The arm action prompts little difficulty, but a

simultaneous and symmetrical leg action does. It must be accepted that, due to the importance it holds as a life-saving stroke, some form of breaststroke, even if it infringes swimming law, must be taught and practised. A teacher will take pains, though, to correct what is legally wrong. It is the feet and the legs which cause difficulty. It taught as a first stroke, as it was for many years, the breaststroke normally takes much longer than dog-paddle, for example, before the learners are swimming. It is a common teaching experience to have non-swimmers off on dog-paddle during the first or second lesson. Breaststroke takes longer, but once the swimmer has the basic skill, progresses is very rapid and in a matter of weeks or months, the swimmer will be achieving long distances.

Conversely, the dog-paddle swimmer with a very early start, will the usually take months before the basic skill is absorbed and longer still to achieve distances. The importance of multi-stroke teaching and of developing that stroke most natural to the individual is obvious. Begin at the rail and transfer the skill to the float, but keep to short distances or even to a limited number of leg kicks. Often a tidy leg kick deteriotates because the learner has been instructed to swim a width, when two or three kicks only were possible.

Demonstrations are more valuable than words. The arm action is usually easily grasped and practised, in shallow water. Arms only, with the legs isolated and immobile, is too difficult for beginners and improvers. Leave it out. Put the arm and leg actions together for a few strokes only, while learning takes place. Swimming on the back, with life-saving leg kick, uses actions relevant to breaststroke. It allows the swimmers to use the eyes to check the leg action and foot position. Breaststrokers will spend a lot of time kicking with a float or board, in order to develop a smooth, tireless leg action. Look for the incorrect leg action which combines a whip kick one leg and a wedge kick with the other, then correct the offending knee. Remember that youngsters might feel needlessly guilty for having an illegal stroke when there is not the remotest chance that competition will involve them. Life-saving comes before laws.

3

RULES OF SWIMMING

POOL

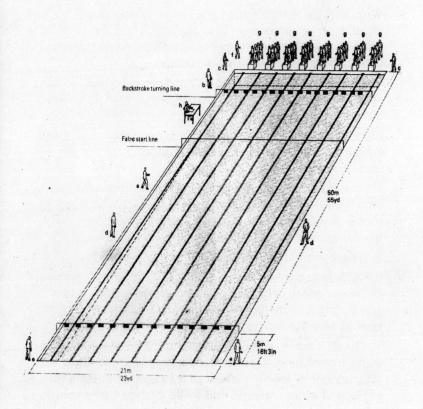

—For Olympic Games and World Championships, Regional Games and all International Competitions specifications for pools are as follows:

Pool should have a length of 50m. When on starting ends or on turning end, touch panels of electronic timing equipment are used, pool should have a length which should ensures a distance of 50 meters between both panels. Against a length of 50 m above surface of water a tolerance of + 0.03m and of 0.8m below surface of water should be there.

Walls

i. These should be parallel and vertical in shape.

With surface of water in a right angle direction end walls should be constructed. End walls should be of solid material with a non-slippery surface, which should extend below surface of water 0.8m.

ii. Along the pool walls rest ledges are permitted, which should be above 1.2m below the surface of water and have a height of 0.15m.

iii. Electronic pads should have a size of atleast 240cm×90cm×1cm which should extend 30 cm above and below the water surface.

To control individually, electronic equipment for each lane should be connected independently. Surface of touch panels should have a bright colour and line markings which should be approved for end walls.

iv. There should be 8 lanes.

v. Each lane should have a width of 2.5m and 2 spaces of 50 cm width which should be outside from lanes 1 and 8. To separate these spaces from lanes 1 and 8 there should be a lane rope.

vi. On all 4 walls of pool, gutter should be placed. If end wall gutters have been installed they should allow for attachment of touch panels at a height of 0.3M above surface of water. Around end walls gutters there should be suitable grill or screen. To keep water at a constant level gutters should be equipped with flexible shut-off valves.

Water Depth

i. /M/ Minimum water depth for competitive swimming shall be 4 feet.

ii. /NC/ 2 meters deep throughout the course. Based on facility availability. Program Operations may waive this requirement for National Championships.

Definitions

EVENTS

In planning any meet, careful consideration must be given the demands to be made upon swimmers, officials, and spectators, in that order. Long, tiresome meets, with too many events and/or entries, often result in keeping small children up late at night. Meets should be planned to terminate within a maximum period of eight hours of competitive events in any one day. Provide adequate meal and rest breaks and sheltered rest areas, properly supervised.

Age Group Events

10-and-Under	11-12 years
50-100-200 Freestyle	50-100-200-400/500 Free style
50-100 Backstroke	50-100 Backstroke
50-100 Breaststroke	50-100 Breaststroke
50-100 Butterfly	50-100 Butterfly
100-200 Individual Medley	100-200 Individual Medley
200 Medley Relay	200-400 Medley Relay
200 Freestyle Relay	200-400 Freestyle Relay

13-14, 15-16, 17-18, 15-18 Years

50-100-200-400/500, 800/1000, 1500/1650 Freestyle

100-200 Backstroke

100-200 Breaststroke

100-200 Butterfly

200-400 Individual Medley

200-400 Medley Relay

200-400-800 Freestyle Relay

Senior Events

The following events for National Championships are recommended for Local Swimming Committee and other championship meets. Eligibility for these championships shall be determined by the LSCs involved.

Long Course Events

50 meters Freestyle

100 meters Freestyle

200 meters Freestyle

400 meters Freestyle Medley

800 meters Freestyle Medley

1500 meters Freestyle

100 meters Backstroke

200 meters Backstroke

100 meters Butterfly

200 meters Butterfly

100 meters Breaststroke

200 meters Breaststroke

200 meters Individual

400 meters Individual

400 meters Freestyle Relay

800 meters Freestyle Relay

400 meters Medley Relay

Short Course Events

50 yd/mtr Freestyle

100 yd/mtr Freestyle

200 yd/mtr Freestyle

500 yd/400 mtr Freestyle Medley

1000 yd/800 mtr Freestyle Medley

1650 yd/1500 mtr Freestyle

200 yd/mtr Butterfly

100 yd/mtr Breaststroke

200 yd/mtr Breaststroke

200 yd/mtr Individual

400 yd/mtr Individual

400 yd/mtr Freestyle Relay

100 yd/mtr Backstroke   800 yd/mtr Freestyle Relay

200 yd/mtr Backstroke   400 yd/mtr Medley Relay

100 yd/mtr Butterfly

BEGIN

Organizers are required to decide which start rule, i.e., one start rule or two start rule should be applied. Whatever start rule is applicable should be mentioned in invitation.

. 1. In one of its decision FINA Bureau declared that one start rule should be applied in 9th FINA World Swimming Championships.

2. With dive Freestyle, Breaststroke, Butterfly and Individual Medley races should start. Swimmers will go to starting platform and remain there as soon as referee blows long whistle. They should take starting position with starter's command take your marks. In starting position they should have 1 foot at front of starting platforms. Position of foot should be taken into consideration only, while position of hand is irrelevant. Starter will give the starting signal when all swimmers are stationary.

3. From water the Backstroke and Medley Relay races should start. Swimmers are required to enter the water as soon as referee blows long whistle for first time. With his second long whistle they should take their starting position. Starter will give the command take your mark when all swimmers have taken their starting positions. Starting signal will be given by starter when all swimmers are stationary.

Backstroke

a. Before starting signal swimmers are required to line up in water facing starting end with both their hands holding the starting grips. They should have their feet under water surface.

They are not allowed to stand in or on the gutter or bend

toes over lip of gutter.

b. At signal for start and after turning swimmer is required to push off and swim upon his back during the whole race. However, he should not do this while executing a turn.

Roll movement of body up to 90° from horizontal can be included in normal position on back. In such event position of head is irrelevant.

Freestyle

a. In such type of competition swimmer is empowered to swim in any style. However, style used by him should be different from used in individual medly or medly relay events.

b. At completion of each length and at finish some part of swimmer's body should touch the wall.

c. Throughout the race some part of swimmer must break the water surface. However, swimmer is not allowed to submerged during turn and for a distance of more than 15 m after start and each turn.

Breaststroke

a. Body should be kept on breast from beginning of first arm stroke after start and after each turn. Swimmers are not permitted to roll onto the back.

b. All arms should be moved at the same time and in same horizontal plane without any change in movement.

c. During propulsive part of the kick feet should be turned in outward direction. Breaking of surface of water with feet after a down-ward dolphin kick is allowed.

d. At each run and at completion of race swimmers should make a touch with both hands at the same time at, above, or below the level of water.

Before touch head should be submerged after last arm pull, if during last complete or incomplete cycle before touch it breaks the water surface at some point.

Butterfly

a. Body should be kept on breast and both shoulders shall be in line with normal water surface from beginning of first arm stroke after start and after each turn. Kicking on side under water is allowed. However, rolling onto back at any time is not permissible.

b. Over water both arms should bring at same time forward and backward.

c. To come to surface a swimmer can have one or more kicks and one arm pull at start and at turns. After start and after each turn swimmer can be submerged completely for a maximum distance of 15 meters. From that point head should have broken the surface. Swimmer is required to be on surface till next turn or finish.

Medley Swimming

—In Individual Medley Events, swimmer is required to cover 4 swimming styles in following sequence:

Backstroke;

Breaststroke;

Butterfly; and

Freestyle.

—4 swimming styles in following order should have to be covered by swimmer:

Backstroke;

Breaststroke;

Butterfly; and

Freestyle.

Timing

a. Officials should be appointed to control Automatic Officiating Equipment. Winner should be selected on basis of time depicted by Automatic Equipment. Placing and time indicated by this equipment should be preferred over decisions of timekeepers. Decision of timekeeper will be taken into account only when this Automatic Equipment is not working properly or swimmer did not activate it.

b. Results should be recorded only to 1/100 of a second when Automatic Equipment is used. To determine time or placement, timing to 3 digit should not be recorded or used when upto 1/1000 of a second it is available.

c. If any swimmer is disqualified during or after an event, it should be specified in official results. However, no time or place should be specified or announced.

Race

a. In Open Water Competitions competitors should stand in water having such a depth from where swimming can be started with start signal.

b. Start positions of players will be decided by draw in such a manner that lowest number should stand on left and highest number on right side.

c. Overhead apparatus or removable equipment at water level should be used to define start line.

d. Starter should be position in such a way that everybody can see him.

e. Start signal should be audible and visual.

f. Men's and women's events should be treated as separate events.

g. Swimmer should end his race in lane from where he started.

h. To qualify swimmer is required to cover whole distance alone.

i. During competition swimmer cannot use any device which help in increasing his speed, buoyancy or endurance.

j. If any member of team, other than swimmer designated to swim enters the water when race is being conducted, whole relay team should be disqualified from the race.

k. A swimmer will not disqualify if he stands on bottom during freestyle events or during freestyle portion of medley events.

Relays

a. Freestyle Relay—Four swimmers on each team, each to swim one-fourth of the prescribed distance using any desired strokes. Freestyle finish rules apply.

b. Medley Relay—Four swimmers on each team, each to swim one-fourth of the prescribed distance continuously in the following order: first, backstroke; second, breaststroke; third, butterfly; and fourth, freestyle. Rules pertaining to each stroke used shall govern where applicable. At the end of each leg, the finish rule for each stroke applies in each case.

Rules Pertaining to Relay Races

i. When automatic relay take-off judging is used, each swimmer must touch the touch plate or pad in his lane at the end of the course to have finished his leg of the relay race.

ii. Any relay team member and his relay team shall be disqualified from a race if a team member other than the swimmer designated to swim that leg shall jump into or enter the pool in the area where the race is being conducted before all swimmers of all teams have finished the race.

iii. No swimmer shall swim more than one leg in any relay event.

iv. In relay races a swimmer other than the first swimmer shall not start until his teammate his concluded his leg.

v. In relay races the team of a swimmer whose feet have lost touch with the starting platform before his preceding teammate touches the wall shall be disqualified.

vi. Each relay team member shall leave the water immediately upon finishing his leg, except the last member.

Finish of Race

a. Rows of buoys should be drawn to indicate area leading to finish apparatus. These lines should be drawn in such a way that they get narrower while near to finish wall. To ensure that only authorised safety craft can enter or cross entrance of finish lane, escort finish lane should be positioned there.

b. As swimmers leave the water, member of medical team is required to inspect them. Swimmer should be provided a chair on which he cant sit during assessment.

c. While leaving water some swimmers may require assistance. Only if any swimmer ask for such assistant should be touched or handled.

d. After getting clearance from medical member, swimmers should be given access to refreshment.

ENTRIES

a. In any combination of aquatic events conducted on a single day at the same site and where preliminaries and finals are held, no swimmer shall be permitted to compete in more than three events per day, exclusive of relays.

b. In meets where a combination of preliminary and final events and timed finals are held, a swimmer may compete in only three individual events per day, unless entered exclusively in timed final events on that day.

c. If a meet or event has no qualifying time standards, swimmers with no established time for an event may enter that event with no submitted time.

d. The above restrictions are effective regardless of the classification mixture and/or that separate meets re being conducted and such limitations shall be clearly stated on the entry blanks.

e. If qualifying time standards are used they may be made in 50 meter course for long course events or 25 yard or 25 meter course for short course events.

f. When timed finals are held, without preliminary heats,

no swimmers shall be permitted to compete in more than 5 events per day exclusive of relays.

OFFICIAL TIME

a. Official time for any swimming event can be achieved only in the relevant stroke/event. Times achieved in a freestyle event can only be recorded as a freestyle time regardless of the stroke used.

b. World records may be established only when timed by completely automatic timing equipment.

c. The official time to establish records, times of record and qualifying time standards can be achieved.

- Official time may be achieved in a USS sanctioned meet or USS approved meet or by one of the following modes:

- As lead-off leg in a relay race.

- In a swim-off held to determine placement in a final event.

- In a time trial or record attempt.

- Split time recorded from the official start to the completion of an initial distance within a longer individual event.

d. It is the meet sponsors' or meet director's responsibility to provide a proper back-up timing system for all events so that swimmers are assured of achieving official times meeting the above requirements.

OFFICIALS AND THEIR DUTIES

Judges of Stroke

a. On each side of pool a judge of stroke should be positioned.

b. They are required to inform referee about any violation of rule. For this they use a signed card on which details of event, lane number, name of swimmer should be clearly specify.

Referee

a. Over all officials the referee have full control. He is

required to approve their assignments, give them instructions for all special features or rules of competitions. It is his duty to conduct play in accordance with rules and decisions of FINA. He will also decide any question which relates to actual conduct of meet, event or competition which does not come under any rule.

b. He can disqualify any player who commits breach of rule.

c. Referee will be responsible to ensure that all necessary officials have placed in their respective posts during competition. If any official is absent or not in a position to act, referee can appoint his substitute, or can appoint additional officials if thinks necessary.

Starter

a. Swimmers are under the control of starter from time they were turned to him till beginning of race.

b. On beginning of event, on side of pool within about 5 metres of starting end of pool, starter should stand. He should stand in such a position that timekeepers and swimmers can easily see and hear the starting signal.

Timekeepers

a. Time taken by a swimmer to complete the race should be noted by timekeepers. Meet Management Committee will certify these watches.

b. With starting signal each timekeeper should start his watch and with completion of race by swimmer to stop it. In races longer than 100 meters they can be instructed by chief timekeeper to record times at intermediate distance.

Chief Timekeeper

He is responsible to provide seating position and lanes to all timekeepers. For each lane 3 timekeepers should be appointed. This number will increase to 5 if no automatic officiating equipment is used. Final time and place should be determined by time if per lane 3 digital watches have been used.

Clerk of Course

It is the duty of clerk of course to assemble all swimmers before event.

Inspectors of Turns

a. At each lane at each end of the pool one inspector of turns should be assigned.

b. They should stand at turning end of pool to record number of laps completed by swimmer in his lane. He is also required to inform player about number of laps incomplete, for which he display a lap card. For this purpose semi-electronic equipment, including under water display can be used.

c. They are required to inform chief inspector of turns about any violation of rules. For this he uses a signed card in which details of event, lane number, name of swimmer, should be specified. Chief inspector of turns will hand over this card to the referee.

Chief Inspector of Turns

Main duty of chief inspect of turns is to ensure that inspector of turns perform their duties properly.

Finish Judges

They should positioned in elevated stands in line with finish from where they clearly see the course and finish line.

Chief Finish Judge

a. Each finish judge will be positioned by chief finish judge.

b. If to judge finish of race automatic officiating equipment is used, he is required to report order of finish recorded by equipment after each race.

Desk Control

Results shown by computer printouts or from results of

time should be checked and placed in each event by chief recorder. He should be the witness of referee's signing the results.

Duties of Officials

Chief Judge

a. Each judge will be put to his position by chief judge.

b. After race he is required to collect signed results from each judge and sent result and placing to Referee.

Race Judge

a. To enable Race judge to see his appointed swimmer he should be placed in an escort safety craft which is assigned by random draw before start of event.

b. Like referee he can order a swimmer from water upon expiry of any time limit.

c. It is his duty to observe that competition is being held in accordance with rules and all breach of rules is being recorded properly and reported to referee.

Turn Judges

a. To ensure that all swimmers execute alterations in course indicated by competition information documents and pre-race briefing, turn judges are appointed.

b. Any violation of turn procedure should be recorded by him on record sheet if race judge was informed about such violation by blasts on a whistle.

c. They are required to hand over the signed record sheet to chief judge at completion of event.

Referee

a. By raised flag and short blasts on whistle he should give a signal to swimmers indicating that event is going to be start. In same way he will indicate the flat at starter to indicate that competition should begin.

b. In order to ensure that FINA rules are observed properly he can intervene in competition;

c. He can disqualify any swimmer for breach of any rule.

TEACH YOURSELF SWIMMING

Assistant Referee

a. It is the duty of assistant referee to ensure that in competition all officials are positioned on their respective posts. With approval of referee he can appoint substitute on place of officials who are absent or are not able to perform their duties. In some conditions he can appoint additional official also.

b. He should lot a draw for Race Judges and should allocate them to their respective safety craft.

Starter

a. He should raise a distinctive flag into vertical position as soon as referee gives the signal;

b. He is required to stand in such a position that to all competitions he can see clearly.

Timekeepers

a. With starting signal they are required to start their watches and should stop them with instruction of Chief Timekeeper.

b. After each finish they should record time and number of swimmer on time card and hand it to Chief Timekeeper.

Medical Officer

a. He should ensure that before beginning of competition all competitors have gone thro' gh a medical test and referee and management committee has informed about any person who is found to be unfit to play. On basis of his report referee can stop any person from participating in competition.

b. To referee he should be responsible for all medical aspects which relates to competition and competitors.

c. With safety officer he is required to advise referee if according to them conditions are not suitable for competition and recommend to change course or manner of conducting the competition.

Safety Officer

a. He should be responsible for safety of event to referee.

b. He should check that whole course is safe, suitable and without any obstruction.

c. He should ensure that during competition necessary powered safety crafts have become available. Purpose of these safety crafts is to provide full safety backup to escort safety craft.

Course Officer

a. He should ensure that start and finish areas have marked correctly and equipments have been placed in correct position.

b. Before start of competition he is required to ensure and inform assistant referee whether or not turn judges are in proper position or not.

c. For correct survey of course he will be answerable to Management Committee.

Recorder

He is required to record withdrawals from competition, to enter results on official forms, and to maintain record for team awards.

Finish Judge

a. They should be placed in line with finish where they should remain to see finish clearly.

b. According to assignment given they should record after each finish placing of swimmers.

GUIDELINES FOR COSTUME

i. Insignia—No swimmer shall be allowed to wear the insignia and/or name of any club or organization which he is not entitled to represent in open competition. He shall be permitted to wear the insignia and/or name of the organization he represents and he may wear the insignia of National Federation or Organizing Committee for Olympic, World continental or Regional Championships.

ii. Design— No swimmer shall be allowed to wear the insignia and/or name of any club or organization which he is not entitled to represent in open competition. He shall be permitted to wear the insignia and/or name of the organization he represents and he may wear the insignia of National Federation or Organizing Committees for Olympic, World, Continental or Regional Championships.

iii. Advertising

- In the competition venue or complex of all events conducted by and under the control of the Corporation or any LSC or division thereof, no swimsuit shall carry any visible marque or insignia in the form of advertising or any words or numbers other than the trademark on technical equipment or clothing, that is in excess of 16 sq.cm in area. A trademark may be repeated provided a name is used only once on a suit. Offenders may be barred from competition under this rule, until they appear properly costumed.

- Products involving tobacco, alcohol or pharmaceuticals containing drugs banned under IOC or FINA rules may not be advertised , but the advertiser's name only may be used.

SCORING

A. Individual events:

4-lane pools: 5-3-2-1

5-lane pools: 6-4-3-2-1

6-lane pools: 7-5-4-3-2-1

7-lane pools: 8-6-5-4-3-2-1

8-lane pools: 9-7-6-5-4-3-2-1

9-lane pools: 10-8-7-6-5-4-3-2-1

10-lane pools: 11-9-8-7-6-5-4-3-2-1

Individual point values shall be doubled for relays. When consolations and championship finals are swum, scoring shall be as follows:

Individual events:

6-lane pools:

final: 16-13-12-11-10-9

consolation: 7-5-4-3-2-1

7-lane pools:

final: 18-15-14-13-12-11-10

consolation: 8-6-5-4-3-2-1

8-lane pools:

final: 20-17-16-15-14-13-12-11

consolation: 9-7-6-5-4-3-2-1

9-lane pools:

final: 22-19-18-17-16-15-14-13-12

consolation: 10-8-7-6-5-4-3-2-1

10-lane pools:

final: 24-21-20-19-18-17-16-15-14-13

consolation: 11-9-8-7-6-5-4-3-2-1

Individual point values shall be doubled for relays, even when relays are swum as timed finals.

B. Triangular meets

Individual events: 6-4-3-2-1-0

Relays: 8-4-0

C. Dual meets

Individual events: 5-3-1-0

Relays: 7-0

AWARDS

When two or more swimmers tie for any place, duplicate awards shall be given to each of such tied swimmers. In such cases no awards shall be given for the place or places immediately following the tied positions. If two tie for 1st place, no award for 2nd place; if three tie for 1st place, no awards for 2nd, 3rd, and so on.

DISQUALIFICATIONS

a. The Referee or designated official making a disqualification shall make every reasonable effort to seek out the swimmer or his coach and inform him as to the reason for the disqualification.

b. Should a foul endanger the chance of success of a swimmer, the Referee may allow him to swim in the next round, or should the foul occur in the final he may order it re-swum. In case of collusion to foul another swimmer, the Referee may, at his discretion, disqualify the swimmer for whose aid the foul was committed, as well as the swimmer doing the fouling.

c. Dipping goggles in the water or splashing water on the competitor's face or body prior to his next event shall not be considered as entering the pool unless the Referee finds that such action is interfering with the competition.

d. Any swimmer who acts in an unsportsmanlike manner may be considered for disciplinary action, at the discretion of the Referee.

e. Obstructing another swimmer by swimming across or otherwise interfering shall disqualify the offender, subject to the discretion of the Referee.

f. A swimmer must start and finish the race in his assigned lane.

g. The time and/or place of any swimmer or relay team disqualified either during or following an event shall not be recorded in the results of that event. If awards have been made prior to the decision to disqualify they shall be returned and made to the proper recipients and if points have been scored by those disqualified the event shall be rescored.

h. No swimmer is permitted to wear or use any device or substance to help his speed or buoyancy during a race. Goggles can be worn, and rubdown oil applied if not considered excessive by the Referee.

i. A disqualification can be made only by the official within whose jurisdiction the infraction has been committed.

j. Any swimmer not entered in a race who enters the pool or course in the area in which said race is being conducted before all swimmers therein have completed the race shall be barred from the next individual event in which he is entered on that day or the next meet day, whichever is first.

k. Coaches having entrants in any event of the program shall not be allowed in the immediate starting area of swimming pools, which must be clearly marked, during the progress of any competition. Upon being apprised of a violation of this rule, it shall be the duty of the Referee to remove, or have such offender removed, immediately. Coaching of swimmers during the progress of an event shall not be permitted. It shall be permissible for coaches or other to signal intermediate times to a swimmer during competition, and this shall not be considered as "coaching".

l. Standing on the bottom during a freestyle race shall not disqualify a swimmer, but he must not leave the pool, or walk, or spring from the bottom.

m. Time and/or place officially recorded for a swimmer shall not be nullified for violations occurring subsequent to such performance.

LANE ASSIGNMENTS—SEEDING—COUNTERS

a. Preliminary Heats When Finals are Scheduled—In order to assure seeded position, the best competitive times of all entries must be submitted. These times shall be assembled by the meet committee with the fastest swimmer first and the slowest swimmer last. Swimmers whose submitted times are identical should be assigned places in the list by draw. Swimmers with not submitted times shall be considered the slowest and shall be placed at the end of the list by draw. Swimmers shall be placed in heats according to submitted times in the following manner:

Three heats- The fastest swimmer shall be placed in the third heat, next fastest in the second, next in the first. The fourth fastest swimmer shall be placed in the third heat, the fifth in the second heat, and the sixth fastest in the first heat, the seventh fastest in the third heat, etc.

Fewer than three heats—(i) If one heat, it may be seeded as a final heat and swum only during the final session, at the Referee's discretion.

If two heats, the fastest swimmer shall seeded in the second heat, next fastest in the first heat, next fastest in the second heat, next in the first heat, next in the second heat, next in the first heat, etc.

Exception— When thee are two or more heats in an event, there shall be a minimum of three swimmers seeded into any one preliminary heat, but subsequent scratches may reduce the number of swimmers in such heat to less than three.

Four heats or more—The last three heats of an event shall be seeded in accordance with (a) above. The heat preceding the last three heats shall consist of the next fastest swimmers; the heat preceding the last four heats shall consist of the next fastest swimmers, etc. Lanes shall be assigned in descending order of submitted times within each heat.

Swim-Offs— A swim-off is considered to be part of the total preliminary process of qualifying for the finals. In no case may a swimmer with a faster time displace another who placed ahead of him within a heat according to the ballot system. If this situation results in disputed qualifications, all swimmers having times field or within the disputed times shall swim-off to qualify for the disputed place or places in the final. The swim-off will be swum with three watches and two judges on each of the swimmers' lanes and the ballot system or modified ballot system shall be used to determine the order of finish, except when automatic officiating equipment is used and is properly functioning.

The official time for the swimmers involved shall be the time set in the original preliminary heat. This elimination may be held at any time set by the Referee, but not more than 45 minutes after the last heat of any event in which any one of these swimmers is competing in that session. In the case of a disqualification in a swim-off the swimmer so disqualified is relegated to the lowest qualifying position for which he is competing. Disqualification in a swim-off for a qualifying position in the championship finals shall not eliminate a swimmer from eligibility to compete in the accompanying consolation finals.

If disqualification leaves a vacancy for the full complement of finalists, swim-offs shall be continued among the disqualified swimmers until a full complement of finalists is assured.

Time Finals

Places-In timed finals, places shall be determined on a time basis, subject to the order of finish within each heat and based upon the ranking system used at the meet. Any ties resulting from the procedure used shall be declared officially tied for awards and points, with no further attempt at resolution.

Heats- In order to assure seeded positions, the best competitive times of all entries must be submitted. The last heat shall be composed of the swimmers with the fastest submitted times, the next to last heat composed of the next fastest swimmers, etc. Lanes shall be assigned in descending order of submitted times within each heat. When there are two or more heats there shall be a minimum of three swimmers or relay teams seeded into the first heat. The last heat should be a fully heat, but the requirement of seeding three swimmers or relay teams into the first heat may result in failure to fill the last heat.

Finals- In finals, the times to be considered are those times made in preliminary heats. If an qualifying swimmers have the same time their respective lanes shall be determined by draw. Lane assignments shall be made in descending order of qualifying times according to lanes.

Counters

Verbal counters shall be limited to one per swimmer, shall be stationed at the end of the course opposite the starting end, and may not coach or aid the swimmer in any way except that they may use watches and signal intermediate times to the swimmer.

The count may be in ascending or descending order.

A swimmer in any individual swimming event of 400 yards or meters or more, except the individual medley, may appoint one counter to call lengths or indicate lengths by visual sign.

In the event of official or counter error it is the responsibility of the swimmer to complete the prescribed distance.

If visual counters are used, they may be stationed at the end of the course opposite the starting end. Visual counters may be lowered into the water at the end of the swimmer's lane, provided that, in the opinion of the Referee, they neither physically aid the swimmer nor interfere with another competitor or present any safety hazard.

Seeding of 50 meter events in a 50 meter course-50 meter events swum in a 50 meter course shall be seeded as provided above. If the event is started at the turning end of the course no change in the lane assignments shall be made, i.e., the slowest swimmer in the heat will swim in the right outside lane.

Distance Events- In 1000/1650 yard and 800/1500

meter freestyle events, the normal order of heats may be reversed by swimming the fastest heats first and alternating women's and men's heats. The meet announcement shall state the order of heats for these events.

Change of Program and Postponement

-The order of events, as laid down in the official program, shall not be changed. The announced arrangement of heats in any event shall not be added to or altered, except by the authority of the Referee, to the extent of consolidating the heats.

Postponement or Cancellation

-If, prior to its commencement, unusual or severe weather conditions preclude the possibility of safely and effectively conducting a meet, the meet committee may cancel or postpone it.

- Should a meet have actually commenced, and in judgement of the Referee cannot safely and effectively continue because of unusual or severe weather conditions, or for some other compelling reason, the Referee, in his sole discretion, may suspend the meet or any particular event until conditions warrant continuance. If circumstances do not warrant continuance, the Referee may cancel the meet or postpone it to a further date or time, with the approval of the meet committee.

- At the Meet Referee's discretion, individual events 200 yards/meters or longer or any relay event may be combined by age, sex and/or distance provided there is at least one empty lane between any such combination. Stroked may not be combined.

- Entry fees for teams or swimmers may be refunded, in whole or part, at the discretion of the meet committee, upon cancellation of a meet or particular event. The decision of the meet committee on refunding may be appealed to the LSC Review Section.